DATE DUE

Demco, Inc. 38-293

OUTDOOR ADVENTURES
CAMPING

JULIE K. LUNDGREN

ROURKE PUBLISHING

Vero Beach, Florida 32964

110509

© 2010 Rourke Publishing LLC

www.rourkepublishing.com

Photo credits: Cover © Morgan Lane Photography; Title Page © Andrei Marincas; Page 4 © Gorilla; Page 5 © PhotoSky 4t com; Page 6 © Volkova Anna; Page 7 © Morgan Lane Photography; Page 8 © Steve Stedman; Page 9 © Nathan Doctor; Page 10 © David P. Lewis; Page 11 © photo25th, Tatiana Popova, Sony Ho, Marek CECH, maxp; Page 12 © Marc Dietrich, Feng Yu, Darryl Brooks; Page 13 © Robert Churchill; Page 14 © Jeff Banke; Page 15 © Cheryl Casey; Page 17 © Rob Byron; Page 18 © Taily, Miguel Angel Salinas Salinas, Vallentin Vassileff; Page 19 © Dan Roundhill; Page 20 © andipantz, SasPartout; Page 21 © ZTS; Page 22 © Kokhanchikov

Editor: Meg Greve

Cover and page design by Nicola Stratford, Blue Door Publishing

Library of Congress Cataloging-in-Publication Data

Lundgren, Julie K.
  Camping / Julie K Lundgren.
      p. cm. -- (Outdoor adventures)
  Includes index.
  ISBN 978-1-60694-367-0
  1. Camping--Juvenile literature. I. Title.
  GV191.7.L86 2010

  796.54--dc22

                        2009007140

Printed in the USA

www.rourkepublishing.com - rourke@rourkepublishing.com
Post Office Box 643328 Vero Beach, Florida 32964

CONTENTS

THE GREAT OUTDOORS

People camp for many reasons. Some like to enjoy nature and relax, while others want to test their survival skills or travel. Camping can be as simple as pitching a tent in the backyard or as challenging as two or three weeks in the wilderness.

Campers of all ages and abilities can enjoy the outdoors.

Early in human history, people hunted animals and gathered plants for food, shelter, and medicine. As life became more modern, people wished to carry on the traditions and skills that connected them with nature. Camps and camping represent that old connection.

Campers learn new skills, go for hikes, enjoy starry skies, and learn about the land and the plants and animals that live there. They may spend time with friends, meet new ones, or savor peace and quiet.

A cloudless night in a **remote** area offers fantastic sky watching opportunities. Stars, planets, and the Milky Way galaxy can all be seen with just your eyes. Bring a star map to identify different objects, or just lay back and enjoy the show.

TOP TIP
Challenge yourself to learn a new skill each trip. Knowing how to tie knots, read a map, and identify animal tracks make camping more enjoyable.

GET READY

Camping trips are more fun when everyone helps plan where to go and the activities. Consider people's abilities and experience. The more wild and distant the location, the greater the skills needed to take care of yourself and others.

State parks often have **campsites** with electricity, running water, flush toilets, and showers. Call ahead to reserve a site in popular campgrounds. Many places allow campers to make reservations up to a year ahead of time.

Some campsites are just an empty open space, while others might come with a space for a fire or a picnic table.

Wilderness campers must have the skills to handle accidents, sudden changes in weather, and other unexpected events. Help may be days away.

Using a list, pack **gear**, clothes, and food that make sense for the season, the length of the trip, and the planned activities. Driving to the campsite allows campers to bring a few extras, while those canoeing or walking pack only essentials for ease of travel.

Be sure to clean your equipment before each trip and make needed repairs. Then set up your tent to check for missing parts or damage. Borrow or rent any gear you don't own.

Denim jeans do not belong on a camping trip. Once wet, they lose their ability to keep you warm and take a long time to dry. Instead, choose clothing made from **synthetics** or wool.

BASIC CAMPING LIST

Sleeping:
- tent and plastic liner
- sleeping bag and pad
- waterproof rain **tarp** and nylon rope

Personal items:
- change of clothes, including long pants
- sweater
- jacket or windbreaker
- rain gear, including coat and pants
- sun hat and winter cap
- sturdy shoes (wear them)
- sunscreen, sunglasses, lip balm
- toothbrush, toothpaste, bar soap, towel
- insect **repellent**
- water bottle and small day pack

Tools:
- flashlight with fresh batteries
- map and compass
- first aid kit, duct tape, safety pins, and whistle

Cooking:
- camp stove with fuel, matches
- one or two cooking pots and large spoon
- sharp knife, wrapped or protected
- cup for cold or hot drinks, spoon, and bowl
- wash basin, dish soap, and dish cloth
- container, with water

Fun Extras:
- camera
- journal and pencil
- binoculars and field guides
- swimsuit, card game, or camp chair

Pack enough food for the number of people and the number of days of the trip. Dry food weighs less than canned food and takes less space.

Trail mix boosts the energy of hungry campers in need of a snack. To make trail mix, combine dried fruits like raisins, apricots, cranberries, or banana chips with dry cereal, candy, and nuts. Beware of adding chocolate chips. They could melt.

MENU IDEAS INCLUDE:

noodles, soup mixes
tuna
bagels, pita bread
peanut butter
oatmeal
potatoes
cookies
powdered drinks

No refrigeration needed!

SET UP CAMP

Although it is tempting to play and explore upon arrival, set up camp while it is still daylight. Most campsites have a flat place for the tent and a **fire ring**. Pitch the tent, find water, and gather firewood, if the park allows it.

TOP TIP

Campfires may not always be allowed in state and national parks and forests. Dry and windy weather increase the chance of a wild fire. Parks often have a sign letting campers know if fire danger is low, medium, or high.

Give everyone a job to make setting up camp quick and fun.

15

CAMP KITCHEN

Nutritious yet simple meals keep everyone fueled for fun. Cooking over a campfire takes patience and skill. Many campers prepare cold meals or use a camp stove for breakfast and lunch, and save the campfire for the evening meal when they have more time. The best cooking fires glow with hot coals, not leaping flames.

TOP TIP

Only prepare the amount of food you think your group can eat. Store leftovers in sealable plastic bags to take back home. Burning or burying uneaten food attracts bears and other animals. Animals that learn they can find regular meals at campsites become pests, or even dangerous.

S'mores remain a favorite camp dessert. To make s'mores, sandwich a piece of chocolate bar and a hot, roasted marshmallow between two graham crackers.

Fire rings help prevent forest fires by keeping fire contained. The fire inside heats the ring, so remember not to touch it until the fire has

When camping in bear country, protect food supplies by storing them where bears cannot reach. Sometimes campground managers provide a special metal box at each site for this purpose. Food, drinks, garbage, pet food, toothpaste, and lip balm all attract bears.

Another way to protect food is to hang the food pack from a rope over a tree branch at least ten feet (3 meters) from the ground and the same distance from the tree trunk.

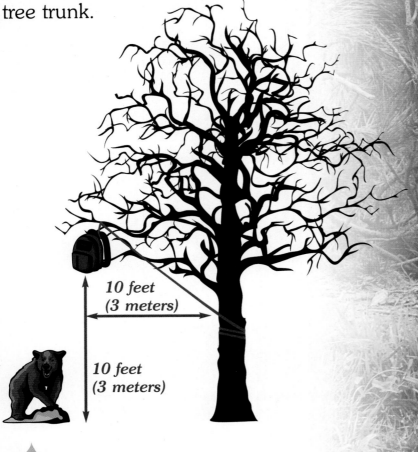

10 feet (3 meters)

10 feet (3 meters)

TOP TIP

Bears have a knack for sniffing out food. Never store it in the tent. Each evening, clean up your camp to avoid unwanted visitors. If you see a bear, do not feed or approach it.

SAFETY

Wash tick bites and apply antibiotic cream. Report any redness around the bite area to your doctor. Ticks can carry disease.

Be prepared for challenges and they will not ruin your fun. Know how to identify plants like poison ivy. Apply insect repellent and cover up with clothing if biting insects get bad. Tuck pants into socks to protect against **ticks**. Check for them daily, especially behind ears and the back of your head. Prevent sunburn by applying sunscreen several times a day.

Identify poison ivy by its shiny green leaves, three per stem.

20

Learn how and when to use the items in the first aid kit. Commonly used items include tweezers for tick removal, **calamine lotion** for rashes and bug bites, and bandage strips and antibiotic cream for cuts and scrapes.

TOP TIP

Drink plenty of water! Dehydration, a condition caused by not drinking enough water, can sneak up on a busy camper. One of the first symptoms of dehydration is feeling thirsty. More serious symptoms include headaches and vomiting.

Camping and other outdoor activities help people develop an understanding of the natural world and respect for the Earth. As campers gain experience, they also gain confidence in themselves and their abilities. Pitch a tent and get ready for a lifetime of camping fun!

TOP TIP

Leave the campsite cleaner than you found it.

Glossary

calamine lotion (KAL-uh-mine LOH-shun): a pinkish liquid that soothes itchy skin

campsites (KAMP-sites): places where campers set up their sleeping and eating areas

gear (GIHR): tools or equipment needed for camping, such as a tent and sleeping bag

fire ring (FYR RING): a circle of rocks or a thick metal ring surrounding a fire pit, to prevent flames from spreading

nutritious (noo-TRISH-uhss): healthy food that provides your body with vitamins, minerals, and energy

remote (rih-MOHT): far away from roads, towns, and people

repellent (rih-PELL-uhnt): a spray or cream that causes pests like insects to stay away

synthetics (sihn-THEH-tihks): fabrics, like nylon and polyester fleece, made from plastics and other man-made materials

tarp (TARP): a strong, waterproof sheet or cloth

ticks (TICKS): very small creatures, related to spiders, which attach themselves to people and animals and drink their blood

Index

Websites

www.dnr.state.mn.us/young_naturalists/camping/index.html
www.fs.fed.us/
http://kidshealth.org/parent/firstaid_safe/outdoor/woods.html
www.lovetheoutdoors.com/camping/Tips/Kids.htm
www.recreation.gov/
www.smokeybear.com/

About The Author

Julie K. Lundgren grew up near Lake Superior where she reveled in mucking about in the woods, picking berries, and expanding her rock collection. Her interest in nature led her to a degree in biology. She currently lives in Minnesota with her husband and two sons.